POP PEOPLE

THE OSBOURNES—
BLEEPED!

AN UNAUTHORIZED BIOGRAPHY

POPPEOPLE™

THE OSBOURNES—
BLEEPED!

AN UNAUTHORIZED BIOGRAPHY
By Kord Miller

SCHOLASTIC INC.

New York Toronto London Auckland Sydney
Mexico City New Delhi Hong Kong Buenos Aires

This book is UNAUTHORIZED and not sponsored
by or affiliated with the stars or producers
or anyone involved with the Osbournes.

ISBN 0-439-49169-X

Designed by Peter Koblish
Photo research by Sharon Lennon

12 11 10 9 8 7 6 5 4 3 2 1   2 3 4 5 6 7/0

Printed in the U.S.A.
First printing, November 2002

TABLE OF CONTENTS

CHAPTER ONE
Welcome to Planet Osbourne!

The American TV Nation has a new First Family! A family whose members have captured the imaginations and tickled the funny bones of young Americans. They're the Osbournes, of course, the stars of their own hilarious real-life TV series. They've swept fans away with their antics and attitudes. Dad — aka Ozzy Osbourne — is a rich rock star, and if he's got a concert to play, then his boss, Mom — aka Sharon Osbourne — will take care of the travel plans. Supermom Sharon is savvy, charming, and occasionally outrageous. And the kids, Kelly and Jack Osbourne, are real, quirky, stylish, cool teenagers who fight, laugh, and love music, and each other. They just happen to live in Beverly Hills and hang out in West Hollywood, where all the action is.

Not Even American — But First in Our Hearts Anyhow!

Who doesn't envy them? What's more, this favorite American family isn't even American — they're British citizens and subjects of the queen! They all have minds of their own (yes, Ozzy does have one, although we don't always know where it's gone to!) and don't mind letting everyone know what they're thinking. They don't have to please anyone, and yet they seem to please everyone. Bring on the Osbournes — they rule!

How It All Began

Last year when MTV visited the new Osbourne family home for an episode of *Cribs,* a show that goes into the homes of rock stars, the audience response was "incredible," according to an MTV honcho! So the channel asked the Osbournes if they could focus on their everyday life for an unscripted series. Crews arrived in September 2001 and filmed a few weeks into the new year.

Living with the cameras was an adjustment for the family. Remembering the first days, Kelly has said that she thought early on about using more "ladylike" language, but she soon just started being herself. The cameras became a part of her life, but after a while, she wished they'd just pack up and leave.

But it's been an incredible ride, with lots of ups. Join the ride and learn what's ahead in the TV season to come. In this book you'll find all you ever wanted to know about the Osbournes, America's new royal family! Let's begin with the immediate members of MTV's Osbourne family, starting with the patriarch himself, Ozzy Osbourne.

CHAPTER TWO
Professionally Known As:
Ozzy Osbourne

Ozzy Osbourne's story is larger than life. He is one of rock and roll's biggest and most enduring stars. Since March 5, 2002, he's become one of TV's biggest stars as well. Entertainment columnists rank him among the world's ten most famous celebrities. Born in 1948 in the industrial British city of Birmingham, one of six children, John Michael Osbourne ("Ozzy" was courtesy of schoolmates) remembers a childhood when there were many fights at home (usually about money), two bedrooms for eight people, and in his clothing collection one pair each of shoes, socks, pants, and one jacket. At fifteen, he took his first job, as a plumber's assistant. At the same time, he had his first ambition — to be a plumber. His next ambition, once he heard the Beatles, was to be one of them.

The Early Years

Unfortunately, Ozzy's salary from unclogging drainpipes didn't exactly buy the mid-sixties swinging London lifestyle of a young Paul McCartney or Mick Jagger. So like many a working-class British youth before him, he decided to sing his way to his goal. He'd performed in some classic English operettas while in grade school and found he had an impressive singing voice and a gift for dramatic flair. Ozzy's next step was joining a band. Make that a lot of bands — with embarrassing names like Black Panthers, Music Machine, Approach, Rare Breed, Mythology, The Polka Tulk Blues Band, and Earth. He is best known, however, for the band he formed in the late sixties called Black Sabbath.

Named after a scary 1935 Boris Karloff movie (it was also the title of the band's first single), Black Sabbath was an instant sensation in 1969 and the group that's credited with inventing heavy metal rock. With Ozzy on lead vocals (and harmonica!),

Black Sabbath also included Tony Iommi on guitar, Bill Ward on drums, and Geezer Butler on bass. Some of the songs they are most famous for are "Paranoid," "Snowblind," and "Mama, I'm Coming Home."

That Hall of Fame

Black Sabbath, one of the most influential bands in the history of rock and roll, is not in the Rock and Roll Hall of Fame. How famous are the Moonglows; how rocking is James Taylor? Yet both were inducted years after Black Sabbath became eligible and was passed over. No one can really explain it — some theorize that Ozzy's first group was too much of a "kids' band," like Kiss (also not in the Hall of Fame!), to pass muster with the elitist rock critics and record execs who pick the nominees or with the larger body of voters, whoever they are. Ozzy's no stranger to this kind of disrespect. From the start, Black Sabbath was despised by rock critics and ignored by radio pro-

grammers, who were afraid to touch the sacred imagery that Ozzy has always delighted in making a spectacle of. In 2000, in true Ozzy spirit, he even asked that Black Sabbath be removed from the ballot of potential inductees. "The nomination is meaningless, because it's not voted on by the fans," Ozzy has said. "It's voted on by the supposed elite of the industry and the media, who've never bought an album or concert ticket in their lives, so their vote is totally irrelevant to me." Sabbath and Ozzy have done just fine, selling millions and millions of records without them. And this year, the Hall is in a very embarrassing situation — Ozzy Osbourne, the band's first lead singer, is now MTV's biggest star and money-maker; MTV is a sister company of VH1, which broadcasts the Hall of Fame annual ceremonies and pays lots of money for the privilege. They can't leave Black Sabbath out again, but if the band gets in after all these years, it might look like a fix is in the works. Stay tuned!

Particular attention was paid to Black Sabbath by critics who were concerned with the group's fondness for imagery from religion and the black arts. This brought the band much criticism, but Black Sabbath insisted that these interests reflected nothing more than theatrics. They just wanted to put on a great show. It was during this time that Ozzy started being called the "Prince of Darkness" in the music press. But Ozzy was certainly not the only rock star to come on as a madman on stage — there were Alice Cooper, Iggy Pop, and quite a few others. Ozzy stayed with Black Sabbath for ten years, but after their *Never Say Die* album in 1978, he quit the band. Black Sabbath lived on (with Ronnie James Dio as frontman), but they would never be the same without him. Ozzy, meanwhile, was eager to explore a new musical direction. With renewed ambition, Ozzy decided to go solo. He made his post-Sabbath debut in 1980 with the album titled *Blizzard of Ozz,* a huge commercial success, followed in 1981 by *Diary of a Madman,* also a multimillion seller. Ozzy's first marriage, to Thelma Mayfair, ended that same year, and on July 4, 1982, he married Sharon Arden. Their first child, Aimee Rachel, made her debut on September 2, 1983.

Very Heavy Stuff

Despite a lucrative solo career, life was not without some very heavy moments for Ozzy, especially in the 1980s. Fresh from the overwhelming success of his first solo album, Ozzy's brilliant twenty-six-year-old guitar player, Randy Rhoads, was killed along with Ozzy's seamstress, Rachel Youngblood, in a tragic airplane accident in Leesburg, Florida. Ozzy witnessed the horrible crash and, for some time afterward, his behavior was very erratic — even for Ozzy. In 1981, an incident occurred that has haunted Ozzy's career ever since. You see, there was this story about Ozzy biting off the head of a bat during a show. Rumor or truth? Well, put the rumor mill to rest, because according to the *Rolling Stone Encyclopedia* and other pop music references, Ozzy did *in fact* bite the head off a bat tossed to him by a fan at a Des Moines, Iowa, concert. The incident enraged animal lovers and, since the poor bat bit back, it resulted in a series of rabies shots for Ozzy.

"I'm not a musician," he said to *Rolling*

Stone. "I'm a ham." This "biting" incident, while decidedly cruel, was intended to be gripping theater, but Ozzy had a tendency to get carried away. Fans know from the TV show that Ozzy is certainly an animal lover. A mellowed man by the early nineties, Ozzy embarked on a farewell tour.

In 1996 he began Ozzfest, an annual rockin' romp through Europe and America. The 2002 version of the tour, costarring System of a Down, Rob Zombie, P.O.D., the Drowning Pool, and many other star-level acts, began in Germany in May and ended in September in Dallas, Texas.

Daddy Dearest!

Who'd have dreamed that this once "Prince of Darkness" would have a whole new career playing himself as a lovable TV dad in a weekly "reality situation comedy"? Just as any traditional father would, Ozzy frets about his daughter's dates, grows furious at the possibility that his son has been smoking in his bedroom, teases his dogs, and snores on the couch. And, believe it or not, Ozzy washes the dishes, vacuums, and takes on other household chores.

Some may refer to the gigantic success of the MTV series as an overnight sensation. It's certainly been a sensation, but for Ozzy — and Sharon — it's taken many a night to bring them to a whole new level of superstardom.

CHAPTER THREE
Sharon Osbourne, Supermom

Yes, she did have a life before she became MTV's most famous mom. Sharon Osbourne was born Sharon Arden in England in the 1950s (she hesitates to say exactly what year, but some websites list it as 1956). Her father, Don Arden, was legendary in the entertainment industry, having worked since the age of thirteen as a stand-up comic and song-and-dance man on the British variety circuit. He was a brilliant mimic with a beautiful singing voice who made his name impersonating famous tenors and movie stars.

Don Arden often left his family at home while he went on tour. They lived in a nice house but, although he was talented, his income was not steady. Hence, Sharon recalls unhappy times when the rest of the family would sit alone in the house, with bill collectors knocking at the door.

Unpredictable Dad!

Sharon's parents were Jewish and spoke both Yiddish and English at home. She had one brother, David, and their mother ran the household and helped to manage Dad's unpredictable career. Just like her father, Sharon was known for her wild and sometimes wicked sense of humor and a very outgoing personality. The family together was a boisterous one. After years of living from feast to famine, Don Arden left the stage and started his own business managing other acts. Don soon earned a reputation for being tough and determined and managed such successful acts as the Small Faces.

Sharon and her brother, David, were young teenagers at the time, obsessed with pop music, and they learned that their father's way of doing business was pretty impressive. Doing things his way always seemed to work. After completing school, Sharon went to work as a receptionist in her father's office. She was very bright and had been a decent student. The music business had always been her passion, and her brother's, too. Don hoped to teach his children the business well enough to create a sort of Arden family dynasty. His company at that time was managing two major acts, one of which was Electric Light Orchestra, or ELO, a synthesizer-heavy pop band; the other act was a heavy metal band known as Black Sabbath.

Ozzy Meets Sharon

Ozzy Osbourne, of course, was the lead singer of Black Sabbath, and his reputation for trouble preceded him. At the time, he was in trouble with everyone — the band, management, and all the friends and family he had. It's said that when Sharon first met Ozzy in her father's office she was so terrified of him that she refused to bring a cup of tea into the room where he sat waiting alone for her father.

Sharon was about eighteen at the time she met Ozzy, who was twenty-six. Ozzy was married with a couple of kids, but his marriage was falling apart. Sharon and Ozzy became friends, and she and her father worked closely with him. In 1979, when he left Black Sabbath, his problems were at an all-time high, and Ozzy feared his career was over.

But Don and Sharon didn't give up on him. Don signed Ozzy as a solo performer and took over his management. Sharon introduced Ozzy to Randy Rhoads, the talented guitar player who joined Ozzy's band and worked on the album *Blizzard of Ozz*.

One day in 1981, as the *Rolling Stone Encyclopedia* reports, Sharon brought Ozzy to a meeting of Columbia Records executives who were not entirely convinced that Ozzy had what it took to be a solo star. So Sharon dreamed up a grand entrance for him, costarring a flock of live doves. The guys in suits were impressed, and Ozzy got his record deal! Sharon felt that she could do a better job of managing Ozzy's career than her father's company had done. So she asked her father to turn Ozzy's management over to her. He refused, and Sharon, who'd shrewdly stashed away over a million dollars, proceeded to buy out her father's share of Ozzy Osbourne. People close to the family say that father and daughter have not spoken since.

Mrs. Ozzy Osbourne

On July 4, 1982, Sharon and Ozzy were married. They honeymooned in Japan, where

Ozzy was already a big star. Sharon continued to manage Ozzy's career throughout all his emotional ups and downs and his serious health problems as a result of his well-chronicled battles with substance abuse. They started a family and had three children in three years: Aimee, Kelly, and Jack. The Osbournes moved from house to house, from England to Los Angeles and back, from the city to the country; so often that Sharon says the family has lived in twenty-four houses in all so far! In spite of all the chaos — which includes being on the road with Ozzy's band for months at a time — Sharon has always provided the emotional home base for the family, no matter where they found themselves.

With a staff to do the cooking and cleaning, Sharon is free to do what she does best: look after her husband and kids and decorate her various houses. Her decorating style, like her mothering, can best be described as unconventional. "You haven't cooked for me since I was, like, seven years old," Kelly complained in the course of one episode. "Things are going to change around here," Sharon replied, but what she had in mind is, so far, unclear!

Sharon in Charge

Sharon has taken over responsibility for just about every aspect of Ozzy's career, right down to the outfits he wears on stage, while assuring him that all he needs to do is "just be Ozzy," which merely generates an enormous amount of money for the family. Sharon has hiring and firing power over every person involved with Ozzy's career, and she is known as a formidable businessperson. Sharon has, over the years, taken on the management of other acts, including indie rockers the Smashing Pumpkins. When Sharon abruptly resigned from managing the Smashing Pumpkins, she stated that it was for medical reasons. "[Lead singer] Billy Corgan was making me sick!" she shouted to the world.

The Tiger

It is this inimitable outspoken style that has earned Sharon her reputation as someone who gets what she wants, and usually on her own terms, just like her father before her. She is very protective of her children and has been compared to a mother tiger protecting her cubs. She defends her family fiercely against any outside attacks and does so in her own irreverent way. When the noisy neighbors were getting out of hand, Sharon first tried to reason with them, and even invited them for a cup of tea. But when threatened by them, she didn't shy away. She's clearly a brilliant negotiator for her own and her family's good. What a mom!

Is It Really "Reality"?

Is The Osbournes *pure reality? Of course not — there are no hidden cameras in the Osbourne mansion, and not one second of tape gets shown on TV without the approval of the show's executive producer — who happens to be Sharon Osbourne! No one as smart as Sharon would let anyone in her family look bad to the world. She makes sure audiences are always laughing with the four stars, and never at them.*

> *One of Sharon's rules is, the children cannot be seen doing anything that might embarrass them — now or later! And it's not just what you don't see, because what you do see is really there very deliberately. It's supposed to make you laugh and cheer and take sides with your new friends who belong to a real / fantasy family. In short, insiders call it great television.*

Sharon's Deal of the Century

The Osbournes is clearly the crown jewel in Sharon's tiara. She brought the show to MTV (inspired in part by an episode of *Cribs* the kids did a year before), and within a few weeks of its airdate it was the most-watched show in MTV's history. It garnered rave reviews from critics. The show was a sensation!

After the Osbourne family's wildly successful first season on the air, MTV asked the family (Sharon, that is) to consider a second season. Trade papers report that Sharon included various unusual demands in the multimillion-dollar contract, such as psychotherapy for all of the Osbournes' household pets. Just looking out for the whole Osbourne clan! It's just another example of her instinct for show business flair, something she has in common with Ozzy. Sharon did finally agree to sign the contract, by the way, but in the outrageous theatrical style that has become her trademark, she jokingly offered to sign it in blood — in true heavy metal fashion. The news came hand in hand with the announcement that Kelly would be making her singing debut on the 2002 MTV Movie Awards show.

Grooving to the Music

Sharon's taste is eclectic. She wears casual oversized T-shirts and capris around the house, then steps out in a stunning pink Chanel suit to visit the queen of England. She listens to everything from Led Zeppelin to opera's Pavarotti. Of course she loves Black Sabbath, but she also loves Vivaldi's "Four Seasons." For the record, when she's on her own, listening to music in her car or at the house with no one around, her favorite band of all is

Queen. As far as new bands go, Sharon says Jack forces her to listen to Tool, but she likes Foo Fighters and Coldplay. In her opinion, a lot of the so-called new young bands are doing something retro, something she's seen and heard before in her many years in the music business as both manager and fan. But she's always looking for something she thinks is really new, so she goes out regularly to hear bands play in Los Angeles.

Supermom!

Sharon attends lots of musical events in her roles as wife and manager of the "Prince of Darkness" and mother of the Osbourne kids, and she's a glamorous celebrity in her own right. But given the choice of attending star-studded parties all over the world or staying home, Sharon says she prefers a quiet night at home! But does she ever relax? Her family says no, never. Ozzy lovingly says Sharon is a lunatic workaholic who works day and night. Sharon says she sleeps about four to five hours a night because she has to get up early to make phone calls to Europe and to get the kids out of bed. She also has an office, although it doesn't looks like a typical one. Her office is often in her home or in the carriage house on the grounds. She loves making deals and arrangements but most of all, she loves her family and has managed to find a unique way to make it all work for her, so that she can do what she loves and spend time with the people she loves. Now that's a Supermom!

CHAPTER FOUR
Princess Kelly

Ozzy and Sharon's second child, Kelly, was born in England on October 27, 1984 — eighteen months after her older sister, Aimee, and thirteen months before the birth of her brother, Jack. So for a while there were three adorable toddlers in the Osbourne household.

The family has lived in small English villages, where the children were sometimes taunted on the way to school about their outrageous father. They've lived in London as well, and have recently relocated to a Spanish-style mansion in Beverly Hills, where they are currently the most famous residents of their already famous neighborhood.

Schooling

Kelly has attended both public and private schools and has had homeschooling from tutors. Like her brother, Kelly has struggled with the reading problem known as dyslexia. What's more, she's often been taken out of school to travel on the road with her father's band — so her education has been an unusual one. Kelly has always had a nanny named Melinda (who's sort of a personal family assistant) to keep things running as smoothly as possible. Luckily for Kelly, she has a loving family and faithful friends who are always around to listen to her problems and opinions — and Kelly seems to have an opinion on just about everything.

An Original

There's never been another teenage character, live or scripted, on television who looks or talks like Kelly Osbourne. She hangs out at the house with the TV cameras rolling, wearing no makeup, in her rolled-waistband sweatpants, her hair in electroshock mode, while she chews her nails, complains, laughs, and whines without a trace of self-consciousness. She'll bop brother Jack over the head, or snuggle up to her father, Ozzy, and plant a kiss on his forehead in front of a delighted camera crew. What a girl! Unlike most girls her age, Kelly doesn't seem to be obsessed with her looks or her weight. While American girls are being bombarded by messages that they have to look a certain way, Kelly is refreshing and confident and refuses to worry about her weight. She told the *London Times,* "My physique goes against everything L.A. stands for." Continuing to explain the reason for her remarkable self-confidence, she added: "I've got my dad's gift for making a fool of myself in public and not caring, and my mum's sense of humor and strength. I guess that's it."

And *that* is pretty cool! Some viewers think that Kelly is the only "sane" member of her famous family. For all her flamboyant fashions, pink hair, and colorful language, Kelly is, after all, a pretty well-adjusted, likable teen, with many of the same problems faced by other, nonfamous girls her age — her brother gets on her nerves, her parents often embarrass her, and she hates math. Nothing so unusual there!

Kelly on the Town

Although Kelly lives in a beautiful house, she likes to socialize and get out around town. After her homework is done, of course, Kelly will hit some Los Angeles hot spots, like the famous rock star mecca the Roxy or the outrageous Standard Hotel. Even surrounded by other celebrities, or the children of celebrities, Kelly stands out. When she walks into a room, she stops traffic. But she's gotten used to that, and soon gets into mingling and mixing just like everybody else.

Kelly's been heard to complain about people in or around her crowd who are pretentious and rude. She likes to think that, unlike many other rich kids, she is not obsessed with money or fashion, although the family money certainly allows her to maintain a fabulous lifestyle. Kelly's passions are shopping, hanging out, and listening to music. She also enjoys being on TV, and though she might roll her eyes at her family's kooky antics, she really adores her parents and her brother. In an interview, Kelly said that her mother is so cool that, if Sharon were eighteen, Kelly would want to hang out with her.

And that's a compliment any mom has to appreciate!

The Pink Suite

Kelly has two whole rooms to herself — a bedroom plus a sitting room with a sleepover couch. Everything in her bedroom is pink, Kelly's signature color. She also has two bathrooms, because she doesn't like other people using her stuff. She retreats to her room when her family and the cameras get to be a bit much for her.

She rearranges the furniture often and changes her collection of chairs the way some people change their shoes. When she sees a new one that she likes better than one she already has, in comes the new and out goes the old! Although she never has enough people over to sit in all her chairs, she can't stop buying more. One of her favorites is from the set of the famous movie *A Clockwork Orange*. And she also has a great bubble chair that hangs from the ceiling.

The Music in Her Life

When a reporter asked Kelly what her favorite CD of all time was, she slyly answered that she couldn't say because she hasn't lived long enough to tell! Give her another twenty years, she added, and ask again! She is cool with the Strokes and Starsailor these days and loves old-timers like Madonna, whose hit single "Papa Don't Preach" was Kelly's *own* first hit song and the one with which she made her MTV debut. At home, Kelly likes to mix old music and new. She'll listen to the White Stripes, then switch to the best of Blondie, from the late seventies, or the pioneering Velvet Underground, a sixties group discovered by the famous artist Andy Warhol. One thing Kelly doesn't like is being blasted by Jack's music, like his favorite new metal bands, coming from speakers all over the house, so that there's no place to escape. Kelly's been surrounded by music all her life, so in spite of her saying that she needs twenty more years to choose her favorite CD, it's clear that she knows what she likes and what she doesn't.

Dad Ozzy is certainly one performer who Kelly's heard lots of during her life. Where some families picnic or go boating together, the Osbournes stage a rock tour and bring everyone along! By the way, Kelly's favorites of her father's songs are "Paranoid" from *Live Evil* and "Crazy Train" from *We Sold Our Soul for Rock and Roll*.

It's no surprise that Kelly is an eager concertgoer. She told *Interview* magazine that she's seen the band Incubus "about 35,000 times." Now *that's* a fan!

Kelly's Style

When Kelly was asked during an Internet chat session if she preferred punk fashion, fifties vintage, or sporty casual style, she answered, "I like the eighties. I'm a little eighties girl. And I've always wanted to design clothes, so later on I may do that."

Kelly is more of a trendsetter than a follower of fashion and always manages to put together her own original look. She told MTV that she doesn't like putting together outfits totally designed by someone else and she doesn't buy into anyone else's idea of how you should look. "I live in L.A.," she said, "surrounded by tall, skinny blonds, which I'll obviously never be, so I've got to work with what I've got."

With her fashion inspirations being Cyndi Lauper and Madonna, Kelly borrows from a wide spectrum of styles and designers. Some of her favorite designers are British original Zandra Rhodes and German minimanlist Helmut Lang. She likes bags by Bloom and lots of things from Dolce & Gabbana, Versus, and Diesel. Among her favorite stores are Barney's and Fred Segal in Los Angeles.

That Hair!

The shade worn by Kelly during her first season on MTV is called Pink Flamingo, from Fudge. She had to take some color out of her naturally light hair to get that vibrant pink, so she uses tons of conditioner to keep her hair soft. She'll apply Kiehl's Silk Groom for softness and a hot oil treatment to keep her scalp healthy. Her spikes are courtesy of Bed Head wax sticks. It's a lot of work to keep her hair bright, shiny, and soft — and healthy as well! As she told MTV, "I don't really care what people think about my hair. It's my hair, so why should they care? Ooh, that rhymed!"

Makeup

Like her dad, Kelly likes MAC's Smolder eyeliner. She's found that Shiseido facial cleansers work well for her, and she babies her skin with a good cleansing ritual. She cleans up breakouts with some Sisley facial pads and MAC toners, and when she's going all the way she uses a lot of eyeliner and some MAC eye shadow. She outlines her mouth with a little lip liner, then fills in with Chanel Infrarouge Whisperlight. A favorite product is Chanel's Crayon Visage Duo Face Colour Pencil, because it works on eyes, lips, and cheeks, which is pretty handy when you have to "do your face" in the back of a limo.

Tattoo

As viewers now know, Kelly has a tattoo of a heart on her hip. She says getting it was a bit of an annoying pain but didn't really hurt — she just wanted to get it over with. Remember how afraid she was that her mom would hit the roof? So she made Ozzy (a walking tattoo museum) tell Sharon, who was upset for a bit, but soon got over it.

Can Kelly Do Just About Anything She Wants?

Kelly says she has lots of freedom because her parents trust her. She told *Interview* magazine, "My parents don't really worry about me because I'm not like the other kids. I'm not easily influenced to do things. I do what I want to and am prepared to pay the consequences."

So Kelly's formula for freedom is: Earn your parents' trust and show them that you're not going to dumbly succumb to peer pressure. Show them you're responsible, and they'll let you do more.

Like everyone else, Kelly doesn't like curfews, but she knows that a phone call, if she's going to be late, is better than having worried parents and a scene when she does get home. Kelly knows that if she wants to follow her dream of having her own musical career, she has to be responsible, do her homework, show up on time, and get along with others, although it may sometimes be a struggle. Where can any girl learn more about being herself and getting along with others than in the amazing Osbourne household?

Are You Bleeping to Me?

The Osbourne clan uses colorful language that most families in America disapprove of and consider rude. In fact, many kids are discouraged from watching the show because of it. MTV handles this issue with the censors by using a bleep noise every time someone swears. If you have premium cable stations like HBO, you might wonder why some channels allow such language and MTV doesn't.

Cable companies across the country may choose to leave MTV off of their basic service should they take offense at the station's programming. This does not apply to pay cable stations. If you pay for HBO, you get HBO. It's like paying to go see a movie. The local cable companies have the upper hand, since they could survive quite well without MTV. MTV, however, could not survive without the cable distributors. Thus, the network has been savvy in making the potentially offensive language a funny part of the show.

CHAPTER FIVE
Jack Sabbath Osbourne, Young Man on the Move

Born November 8, 1985, Jack Sabbath Osbourne was named after his dad Ozzy's band. Although Jack isn't keen on being asked what it's like to be Ozzy's son, Jack Sabbath is a fitting name for this precocious teenager who has been immersed in heavy metal — *music*, that is — since he was a baby.

"My Little Man"

Before he could even walk, little Jack accompanied his dad on his tours around America and the rest of the world. Ozzy would often bring Jack on stage with him and introduce him to his fans. Dad even dedicated his song "My Little Man" to Jack. Although at 5'8" he's not so little anymore, Jack is still his father's "little man." What's more, his unique education is already paying off as Jack carves out his own place in the world of rock and roll. When he's not out on tour, a "typical" day for Jack begins at nine A.M. when Melinda begins to try and wake him. His homeschooling is supposed to begin at ten, but Jack will be the first to tell you that a teenager's brain isn't functional until ten-thirty. Like his dad, Jack suffers from dyslexia and attention deficit disorder. Before he had a home tutor, Jack attended a special school for dyslexic kids. After his studies, Jack works out in the home gym before heading to his job as a talent scout for Epic Records (three days a week). His years of touring with Ozzy have given him an excellent ear for discovering new bands. One band he found already has a development deal at Epic.

"It's a Good Time"

After a hard day's work, Jack likes to play just as hard. One of Jack's favorite sayings is "It's a good time." As he wrote on his MTV online diary, that's "anything that is fun, cool, or exciting." Jack loves playing the drums and is hoping for a soundproof booth to be put in the house so he can practice without adding to the already considerable noise of the Osbourne home. His beloved dog is Lola, who he loves to wrestle and swim in the pool with. Just don't ask him to clean up after her. Going out to rock clubs like the Roxy, the Viper Room, and the Whiskey-a-Go-Go on Los Angeles's Sunset Strip is also "a good time" for Jack, as well as an opportunity for him to spot hot new bands. Jack also likes to hang out with friends in his room. They'll stay up late listening to music, talking, or watching a movie.

Chez Jack

A personal sanctuary and bachelor pad, Jack's room says a lot about who he is. Decorated in dark, masculine colors, it's full of high-tech equipment. He has a TV, VCR, and DVD ("the best invention ever") with surround-sound, and tons of CDs, naturally. He's got a major book collection, too, including a first edition of *Lord of the Rings*.

Jack shares his dad's love of skulls, mixing them with other prized possessions, like a guitar, trophies, and a Chef doll from *South Park*. A prominent place on his shelves is reserved for an Osbourne family portrait. In contrast, Jack's bathroom is very white and bright — the perfect place to showcase his toothbrush collection. "I don't really know why I have so many toothbrushes," he says on one all-Jack website. "It's a good time, though: one for every day of the week." Jack doesn't have a girlfriend yet, but he loves to open up his room to his friends. Jason Dill, one of his best friends, practically moved in. The youngest Osbourne keeps a small and tight-knit group of friends around him. He told MTV that it's hard as the kid of a celebrity (or now, as a celebrity himself) to know who your real friends are. "What makes a good friend is when they start caring — when you're sick and they actually call you and see how you're doing."

On Jack's Shelves

A few of the artists found in Jack's CD collection:

Tool (Aenima, *his all-time favorite*)
System of a Down
Rage Against the Machine
Incubus
TapRoot

> *Hatebreed*
> *Nirvana*
> *Coldplay*
> *Queens of the Stone Age*
> *Kyuss*
> *Nebula*
> *Ugly Kid Joe*
> *Primus*
> *Rob Zombie*
> *Radiohead*
> *Faith No More*
> *Tenacious D*
> *Slipknot*
> *Mudvayne*
>
> *and, of course, tons of Ozzy Osbourne and
> Black Sabbath*

Jack in Black

When it comes to fashion, Jack likes to keep it
simple, just like his old man. (Sister Kelly
seems to have gotten all of their mom's
shopaholic genes.) His favorite color is black,
and he rarely wears anything else. "I wore
black Dickies [basic work slacks] for two
years straight and a black T-shirt," he told

MTV. "I kind of do my own thing." Jack's "nerdy" glasses are also a trademark of his style. He prefers vintage shops — especially for their selection of army surplus — but also speaks highly of the labels Hurley and DVS (then again, they do pay him to wear their clothes on the show). He's become more adventurous in recent months, trading in his curly brown hair for first a bleached-blond Mohawk haircut and later an electric-blue dye job. After all, as Jack said to one hopeful band seeking a label, "You've gotta have good hair to get a deal in development."

Jackfest

When Jack was younger, the annual Ozzfest used to be like summer camp for him. Gradually, though, as Jack has learned more and more about the family business, he has also taken on more responsibility. In past years, Jack has patrolled the crowds and backstage areas with his own camera, and in 2002 he had eighty-five percent of the say of who performed on the Second Stage. A showcase for up-and-coming acts, it's the perfect venue for Jack to develop new bands. With Ozzy claiming that this will be his final year headlining

the heavy metal festival, Jack may well be
running it in a few years.

2002 Ozzfest Second Stage Lineup

*Check out the bands Jack invited to be
part of his dad's high-profile tour:*

Down
Hatebreed
Meshuggah
The Apex Theory
Lostprophets
Pulse Ultra
Neurotica
Chevelle
Ill Niño
Flaw
3rd Strike
Otep
Seether
Andrew W.K.
Mushroomhead
Soil
Glassjaw
The Used
Switched

CHAPTER SIX
What Kind of Parents Are Sharon and Ozzy?

Ozzy and Sharon Osbourne's kids stay out until all hours, come and go as they please, dye their hair crayon colors, get themselves tattoos, and curse like a rock-and-roll road crew. What do Sharon and Ozzy do about all this? Not much, it may appear. They seem to enforce very few of the rules that are standard in most American households. As a matter of fact, they indulge in some of these same antics. They swear just as much as their kids, if not more, dye their hair unnatural colors, get tattoos (Ozzy, at least), and engage in what would normally be considered fairly antisocial behavior. So what kind of parents are they, anyway? Let's take a look at some of their parenting techniques.

Papa Does Preach

Ozzy doesn't exactly lecture his kids in the usual way. He does, however, talk to them very frankly about everything — the dangers of sex, drugs, smoking, and drinking — all the big topics parents are supposed to warn their kids about but don't always know how to handle. Ozzy's style with this is pretty straightforward. Having quit smoking cigarettes after more than forty years, he disapproves of smoking of any kind and absolutely forbids it in the house. He tells them, if they really want to be unique, *don't* get any tattoos, because everyone already has them. He warns his kids not to get caught drinking or taking drugs because they're not American citizens and, as guests of this country, they could be kicked out. He wants to avoid being hypocritical, given his well-known lifelong battles with addiction. But because of his own many outrageous excesses, he tries to give his children the benefit of his experience. He says, "I think being a parent is the most difficult job on the face of the earth. You hate to say things that will upset your kids, but then sometimes

The Osbournes featuring Ozzy, Sharon, Kelly, and Jack is the biggest hit in MTV history.

Osbournes then . . .
(l. to r.) Jack, mom Sharon, Kelly,
firstborn Aimee, and papa Ozzy.

Osbournes now . . .
Sharon, Kelly (blonde!), Ozzy, Aimee and Jack

Mama don't preach —
Kelly and Sharon share a love of
shopping and pets. This is their dog Minnie.

"It's weird. I don't think me or Jack ever thought for a day in our life that this sort of thing would ever happen to us." — Kelly

A fan poses in front of the most famous house on the block. Casa Osbourne!

Jack has become a talent scout for up-and-coming rock bands.

"I'm a mum and this is the kids — and he's the rock star," Sharon says. She makes it sound easy!

"I think we've all pretty much handled it [fame] the same. My kids are doing a pretty good job handling it." — Ozzy

Kelly's "star" is on the rise —
and glittering!

The Osbournes are all about family.

"I love you more than life itself . . . but you're all mad." — Ozzy

you have to because you can't let them run around wild."

She's Heavy. She's Our Mother.

Sharon's the one entrusted with the role of the "heavy" more often than Ozzy. She's the one who insists on the kids having a curfew, because she's the one who can't get to sleep unless they're safe at home. Their curfew is, however, exceptionally reasonable (midnight during the week and two-thirty A.M. on weekends) and can be extended with a well-timed phone call under the right circumstances. Sharon's reasoning is this, as she told MTV in an interview last spring: "I try to treat them as young adults and hope they'll give me back the respect, so if they want to stay out later than curfew then they're not afraid of picking up the phone to say, 'Look, this is what's going on, this is where I want to go, can I go?' Instead of, like, being afraid to pick up the phone and call." This method seems to work pretty effectively, although it is usually Kelly who ends up calling, on her and Jack's behalf, to get a curfew extension. At least Sharon knows where they are and that they're all right and when to expect them. Kelly and Jack know that she cares about them and that if they come home later than agreed upon they are robbing their busy mother of her sleep and there will be a price to pay with her moods. They'd usually rather avoid a flare-up from Sharon.

No Secrets

Sharon and Ozzy talk to Kelly and Jack about everything — the care of the dogs, the working of the vacuum cleaner, the outfit Ozzy's wearing for a show. Sharon also talks extensively, especially with Kelly, about matters of romance. Sharon shared her views on the "birds and the bees" with MTV: "As much as you think you love someone, it's puppy love, it's infatuation, and you've got to take your time. I try to make [her] realize how special [she is] just by being a woman. All women are special." Sharon tries to teach Jack to be responsible and to treat women respectfully. She says, "Sure, there's tons of girls that want to go with Jack because of who [he] is. What I try to tell Jack is to just have respect for that woman because she's a woman like your mom, like your sisters." Ozzy and Sharon have high expectations of their kids, but these don't include getting all A's in school or getting into an Ivy League college or becoming an Olympic athlete. They simply expect their kids to do their best at everything they do and to treat people well. Ozzy understands that school has been difficult for his kids, like it was for him. But he says, "Education's come a long way, and Sharon's done a remarkable job." Sharon's views on schoolwork are very clear. She understands that her children have learning disabilities, but she doesn't let them use that as an excuse to slack off. She has said that she doesn't mind their failing a test as long as they've studied and done their best. Sharon tells Kelly and Jack that it's a waste of their time and everyone else's if they don't try in school. Kelly and Jack are so close in age and have spent so much time together that they should've had a lot of practice in getting along with each other. They drive each other crazy. Their sibling rivalries can sometimes be intense and can disrupt the entire household. At times their parents do intervene, but often they back off to allow Kelly and Jack to work it out themselves. Kelly has a tendency to have teenage temper tantrums,

45

or prolonged whining and sulking sessions, which Ozzy has dubbed her "wobblers." By referring to these freak-outs as "wobblers," Ozzy has actually come up with an ingenious technique. He recognizes and validates Kelly's irrational behavior by giving it a special name, yet at the same time he defuses her anger by giving it a humorous name. How long can you stay mad when you're having another "wobbler"? When it comes to parenting, Ozzy is at times more savvy than he admits.

America's First "Reality TV" Family

Way back in 1972, the Loud family from Santa Barbara, California, allowed a camera crew into their home and into their lives for several months. The three hundred hours of film was shot and edited down into twelve episodes, which ran on PBS stations as An American Family. *The prosperous and attractive Louds, with their five teenage children, became a national sensation. But TV viewers seemed divided between those who were horrified that a family would allow their private lives to be shown on television and those who couldn't get enough. Sound familiar? By the way, reruns and updates of* An American Family *keep popping up — check them out.*

All They Need Is Love

Most important, Kelly and Jack and Sharon and Ozzy quite obviously love one another very much. Ozzy says that he would do anything to make his wife and kids happy. He told *Interview* magazine, "I love my dogs, my kids, my wife, my house. I loved my wife before the [MTV] show and I love her now. To see my wife and children happy, that's all that matters to me." He and Sharon involve their children in almost every aspect of their work and lives and encourage them to follow their own dreams. Kelly wants to sing — her parents help her make it happen. Jack wants to have his own record label — they get him started and guide him. Ozzy and Sharon accept Kelly and Jack exactly as they are and constantly show their children that they are important to them and that they are supportive of their talents. Meanwhile, they have a lot of laughs. What kind of parents do they sound like to you?

A Royal Triumph for Ozzy and Sharon

Music lovers (and reporters) the world over agreed: Ozzy Osbourne stole the show at the June 2002 monster concert celebrating the Golden Jubilee of England's Queen Elizabeth II. When Ozzy came on to sing "Paranoid," hundreds of thousands of fans watching the show live from Buckingham Palace (the queen's official residence) and in the streets of London on giant TV screens chanted, "Ozzy! Ozzy!" Only the queen herself got a bigger ovation. And hundreds of millions of viewers around the world saw the young princes, William and Henry, banging their heads and clapping in time during Ozzy's performance. Other middle-aged British rock stars like Eric Clapton and Joe Cocker got only polite applause from the teenage princes. Even legendary Paul McCartney didn't get the crowd to shout their love for him like Ozzy did.

Hosting the telecast was none other than Sharon Osbourne, whose genuine awe at the event plus her famous sense of humor and perfect timing received unqualified raves. "She's a natural to host next year's Oscars," said the chief of a major TV network — not bad for Sharon's debut as a television emcee!

CHAPTER SEVEN
The Extended Family

If you watch *The Osbournes,* you know that the Osbournes have an extended circle of family and friends who are important to them. Take a look at some of the people who share their lives:

Family
Aimee

At nineteen, she's the oldest child of Sharon and Ozzy. She's a singer and musician, too, like her father and sister, but she's not famous — yet! She may appear in at least a couple of episodes of the second season on MTV, so maybe we'll get to hear some of her music, too. In any case, audiences are looking forward to seeing what she's like! Little is known about her, except that she dated Taylor Hanson (of the band Hanson) for a while, and she does actually appear in a couple of the episodes from season one, only they blur her face out.

Ozzy's Other Kids

Ozzy has other children, from his first marriage, to Thelma Mayfair. He adopted the son she already had, Elliot Kingsley, when he was five. Ozzy and Thelma had two other kids:

Jessica

Jessica Starshine Osbourne, Ozzy's oldest child, likes to keep a low profile. Jess is almost thirty, and she's so shy that she usually goes just by Jessica Starshine to avoid letting people know that her dad is the famous musician. Not much has been publicized about Jess, but how cool would it be if she made an appearance during the second season?

Louis

Louis Jon Osbourne lives in England, where he's a well-known techno DJ. He's twenty-seven and has his own website. He has a shaved head, a good sense of humor, and, according to Sharon, is "a big part of the family."

You can see him in the Christmas episode, and if you're extra-sharp you might catch a glimpse of him in a couple other episodes, too. Can you tell which ones?

Friends
Melinda

Although she's not related by blood, the Osbournes' nanny, Melinda Varga, is definitely a part of the family. She's from Melbourne, Australia — you noticed the accent, right? She's married, and she helps the family out in so many ways beyond her duties as a nanny. Melinda tries to avoid getting too wrapped up in the crazy dramas and arguments in the Osbourne household. When things get too chaotic, she likes to put on her headphones and jam out to her favorite music.

The Woods

The Osbournes have known both Elijah Wood (he played Frodo in *Lord of the Rings*) and his sister, Hannah, for a while, and they both show up at the house sometimes. Elijah even helps clean up a dog mess in one episode — now that's a friend!

Michael

Michael is the security guard they hired to watch the house. Besides walking the grounds and protecting their home, Michael likes playing pool. He also once got mistakenly arrested in back of their house when the Osbournes' neighbors thought he was an intruder!

Robert

Kelly swears he's her "best friend" and not her boyfriend, but he sure is around a lot. The verdict is still out on that one. She obviously adores him, and he went to a lot of trouble to buy her a birthday gift she'd really like.

Jason

Jason Dill is the pro skater who overstayed his welcome at the Osbourne house. He annoyed Ozzy with his constant head-scratching and made Sharon a little angry when he melted a plastic chicken on her stove and didn't even help clean it up! (Yuck!)

Giacomo Osbourne?

"I'm Ozzy Osbourne," the man born John Michael Osbourne says at the end of the first season. "It could be worse . . . I could be Sting."

It could be a lot worse for Jack and Kelly, too, had their parents followed the trend of kid-naming among other rock stars.

Here are a few examples of some rock stars and their unusually named children:

Frank Zappa	Dweezil and Moon Unit
Madonna	Lourdes and Rocco
Cher	Elijah Blue and Chastity
Bob Geldof and Paula Yates	Fifi Trixibelle Peaches Honeyblossom Pixie
Michael Hutchence (INXS) and Paula Yates	Heavenly Hirani and Tiger Lily
Will and Jada Pinkett-Smith	Jaden and Willow
Steven Tyler	Taj
Alice Cooper	Calico
David Bowie	Duncan Zowie

Victoria "Posh Spice" and David Beckham	Brooklyn
Kurt Cobain and Courtney Love	Frances Bean
Grace Slick	God (Later changed to China)
Bono (U2)	Elijah Bob Patricius Guggi Q and Memphis Eve
Michael Jackson	Prince Michael Jackson, Jr. and Paris Michael Katherine Jackson
Sting and Trudie Styler	Giacomo

The Osbourne Zoo

Not all of the members of the extended Osbourne family walk on two legs. In fact, most of them use four! The Osbournes have seven dogs and two cats. Their most famous dogs are Lola, the bulldog who practically gets an entire episode to herself (for pooping in the corner!), and Pipi, a black Pomeranian who got lost for a month but was finally returned. The other dogs are two Japanese Chins named Maggie and New Baby, another Pomeranian named Minnie, a Chihuahua who goes by the name of Martin, and Ozzy's favorite, Lulu. And let's not forget the two cats, Puss and GusGus. Despite having all these animals in their home, the Osbournes aren't necessarily that good at training them — housebreaking Lola seemed an insurmountable challenge. That's why they called in dog therapist Tamara, who claimed to make great progress with their most troublesome dog, Lola — just before she made another puddle on the expensive rug!

CHAPTER EIGHT
Osbourne Astrology

Ozzy: December 3, 1948

It'd be an understatement to say that Ozzy is an unconventional dad. That may be because he's the classic sign of a rock star: Sagittarius. Sagittarians love traveling, which is perfect for someone who spends part of every year on tour. Also, Sagittarians are almost never shy — which is why Ozzy's such a great performer.

Sharon: Who Knows?

Sharon is notoriously closemouthed about her birthday, but judging by her zany, wild take on life, she could be an Aries. This fits in perfectly with Ozzy; since they're both Fire signs, they understand each other.

Kelly: October 27, 1984
Jack: November 8, 1985

Jack and Kelly are both Scorpios. This has a lot to do with why they're unfazed by having the "Prince of Darkness" as a father (unlike their older sister, Aimee, who's a Virgo and much more coy about who her dad is). This also explains why they fight constantly: Scorpios don't like sharing territory. Still, underneath it all, you can tell they love each other dearly.

How would you fit into the Osbourne family, astrologically speaking?

Aries (March 21–April 19)

Although you and Sharon might butt heads every once in a while, you'd understand: She's just being a mom. Although you'd probably try to stay out of the constant bickering that Jack and Kelly seem to revel in, they'd both try to get you on their side, because you're so strong-minded!

Taurus (April 20–May 20)

Unlike Jack and Kelly, who are often a little rude to the Osbourne nanny, Melinda, you'd know how to be nice to her. As a result, you could be sure she'd always stick up for you, no matter what — even when it really was you who threw a bagel in your neighbor's yard. Plus, you'd be good to have around, because you'd never forget important stuff, like feeding the many dogs or letting them out so they could stop doing their business in the house!

Gemini (May 21–June 20)

This family could sure benefit from your ability to put yourself in someone else's shoes. All those people who get into spats with the Osbournes, like those rude neighbors, would appreciate your perspective on things. Maybe you could even get Ozzy to stop throwing firewood through people's windows! And when one of Jack's friends overstayed his welcome, you'd be good at letting him know without hurting anyone's feelings.

Cancer (June 21–July 22)

You'd be as thick as thieves with either Kelly or Jack (but probably not both, since they fight so much). Cancers are supersensitive, so they can tell how much they can get away with and when it's time to call it quits. Everyone in this family could benefit from your kindness and practical skills. If you know how to make a grilled cheese sandwich or pop popcorn, you'd be a treasured asset.

Leo (July 23–Aug. 22)

Just what the family needs, another superstar! Luckily for you, it seems the Osbourne family's spotlight is always wide and bright enough so that everyone gets a chance to shine. And you can be sure that everyone would do their best to support you in whatever you decided to do: Just look at how much energy they all put into Kelly's musical career! Meanwhile, I know you'd be a great friend to have cheering backstage when each of the other Osbournes was taking their turn in the spotlight.

Virgo (Aug. 23–Sept. 22)

If you lived in this family, they certainly wouldn't need to hire trainers for their dogs and cats. Before long, the Osbourne zoo would be following you around, and there wouldn't be any more embarrassing accidents in the house, that's for sure. You'd save the Osbournes a fortune on pet therapists. Although you might occasionally get annoyed about having your life captured on film, you'd probably get used to it and even learn how to have fun, in spite of the camera crews.

Libra (Sept. 23–Oct. 22)

The Osbournes have a very individualistic style. But you could definitely lend a little class to their house. Although you might be embarrassed when they start blasting Sabbath out the windows, you'd always be there to smooth things over the next day. And none of your friends would overstay their welcome or melt anything on the kitchen griddle.

Scorpio (Oct. 23–Nov. 21)

Just what this family needs, another Scorpio! Scorpios often need a lot of space, because they're very individualistic people. You like having privacy and room to grow. Ultimately, you'd do fine with these guys, as long as you had your own bedroom and bathroom (Kelly has two bathrooms to herself!). Although there'd definitely be run-ins with the other Scorpios in the house, Jack and Kelly, you'd also have the benefit of really understanding each other. How many brothers and sisters can say that?

Sagittarius (Nov. 22–Dec. 21)

Although you and Ozzy would be different in almost every way (Let's face it: There's no one quite like him, is there?), the benefit of being the same sun sign would mean that you'd always "get" him, even when he's being really mumbly and weird. You could act as a translator for the rest of the family — which could really come in handy those times when no one seems to know what Ozzy's talking about.

Capricorn (Dec. 22–Jan. 19)

Whenever you got woken up in the middle of the night by Jack blasting heavy metal music out the windows, you'd be pretty mad. But most of the time, you'd feel lucky to live in such an exciting family. Usually, you'd probably just shake your head and laugh at all their ridiculous antics, but every once in a while you might try to talk some sense into them. And if that didn't work, you'd probably just throw up your hands and join in!

Aquarius (Jan. 20–Feb. 18)

Maybe the Osbournes are lucky that you're not in their family: With a mind as creative as yours around, who knows what kind of trouble they'd get into? Also, since you're so good at keeping secrets, you'd be in a lot of the family's plots. Kelly would take you with her to get a tattoo, or maybe Jack would share his CD collection with you.

Pisces (Feb. 19–March 20)

Some people might think you tender Pisceans would be too sensitive for a house as wild and rude as the Osbournes'. But you'd actually be perfect for it, because Pisceans are the most adaptable of all signs. Although you might be reluctant to scream at the slightest provocation when the rest of the family did, it probably wouldn't faze you too much, either. And having your kind presence around would always be a good way for people to soothe their frayed nerves.

CHAPTER NINE
What's Your Ozz -Q?

A tricky test of your knowledge of obscure Osbourne lore . . .

1) Jack's bulldog Lola is named after
   a) Lola Falana
   b) Madonna's daughter, Lourdes
   c) Gina Lollabrigida
   d) The title of a classic Kinks song

2) What food can every member of the Osbourne family prepare?
   a) Steven Tyler's "Trout Meuniere"
   b) Humble pie
   c) Alpo
   d) Microwave popcorn

3) At a June concert, for what very, very famous celebrity did Ozzy have the honor to perform?

a) Queen Elizabeth II
b) The Pope
c) Mike Tyson
d) Liza Minnelli

4) Ozzy's favorite musician is
a) Beethoven
b) Stevie Wonder
c) Paul McCartney
d) Posh Spice

5) Ozzy told which celebrity that he was happy the celebrity got out of his recent legal troubles?
a) Bo Diddley
b) Sean Combs
c) Sean John
d) Puff Daddy

6) What celebrity did Ozzy take photos with in episode three?
a) P. Diddy
b) Dee Dee Ramone
c) Puffy
d) Buffy St. Marie

7) What famous team composed some of the musical shows that Ozzy appeared in as a child?
a) Gilbert and Sullivan
b) Dolce & Gabbana

c) Marks and Spenser

d) Simon and Garfunkel

8) What famous prince jumped up and down during a recent performance of Ozzy's in London?

a) Freddy Prinze, Jr.

b) The Artist Formerly Known As Prince

c) Prince William of England

d) The Prince of Darkness

9) In the outfit Ozzy wears for the video in episode five, he looks most like

a) Dame Edna Everage

b) Lorna Luft

c) Scarlett O'Hara

d) Christina Aguilera

10) Which of the following bands was on Jack's Second Stage in the 2002 Ozzfest?

a) The Carpenters

b) Meshuggah

c) Deep Purple

d) 'N Sync

Answers: 1d; 2c; 3a; 4c; 5b, c, or d; 6a; 7a; 8c; 9d; 10b.

Give yourself five points for each correct answer and a bonus of ten if you picked all three correct answers to number five!

How'd you do?
65 — You *still* need this book, maybe more than ever!
51–64 — Go back and think seriously about the ones you missed!
36–50 — Go back and spend some more quality time in front of your TV!
25–35 — You probably made some lucky guesses.
0–24 — Brain rot becomes you!

CHAPTER TEN
Facts 'n' Stats

Ozzy's Bits and Bites

Basics

Real name: John Michael Osbourne
Nicknames: Ozzy, Prince of Darkness
Birthday: December 3, 1948
Birthplace: Birmingham, England
Childhood residence: 14 Lodge Road, Aston, Birmingham, England
Current U.S. residence: Beverly Hills, CA
Current British residence: A 100-year-old farmhouse called Welders House in Jordans, England — it's about 40 minutes from London

Height: 5' 10"

Weight: 160 lbs

Parents: John and Lillian Osbourne (John was a tool maker and Lillian worked in a Lucas car factory)

Siblings: Brother Paul and Tony; sisters Jean, Iris, and Gillian

Wife: Sharon Osbourne

Children: Aimee, Kelly, Jack (Ozzy also has children from his first marriage to Thelma Mayfair — adopted son Elliot, Jessica Starshine, and Louis)

Wedding to Sharon: In Maui, Hawaii on July 4, 1982

Honeymoon with Sharon: Japan

Instrument: Harmonica

First tattoo: O-Z-Z-Y across his fingers

Faves

Color: Black

Band: The Beatles

All-time musician: Paul McCartney

Neighbor: 1950s–1960s teen idol singer Pat Boone — Ozzy says, "You may say that Pat Boone is a nerd, but he was a great neighbor."

Artwork: Skulls and crosses — there are hundreds of them in the Osbourne house
TV watching partner: Michael, the family security guard
TV channel: The History Channel
Coffee addition: French vanilla-flavored Cremora
Soda: Diet Coke
Skin cleanser: Osea's Ocean Cleansing Mudd
Cologne: Czech & Speake No. 88 ($92 a bottle)
Room in the Osbourne house: The kitchen
Sunglasses: Lunor 1 makes his signature blue shades

Sharon's Boutique

Basics

Real name: Sharon Arden Osbourne
Birthday: 1952
Birthplace: London, England
Current residence: Beverly Hills, CA
Height: 5' 2"
Parents: Father, Don Arden (legendary British rock manager), mom Hope Arden

Siblings: Brother David
Husband: Ozzy Osbourne
Children: Aimee, Kelly, Jack
Dogs: 2 Pomeranians, Minnie and Pippy; 2 Japanese Chins, Maggie and New Baby; 2 Chihuahuas, Martin Bianco and Lulu; bull terrier, Lola; cats, Puss and GusGus
Job: Music manager — she has been Ozzy's manager since 1982 (she has also managed Smashing Pumpkins, Lita Ford, Coal Chamber, Quireboys, Gary Moore)

Faves

Color: Black
Bands: All-time favorite — Queen; but also Black Sabbath, Led Zeppelin (Sharon also loves classical music)
Classical singer: Pavarotti
Classical composition: Vivaldi's "Four Seasons"
Song: John Lennon's "Imagine" — it was Sharon and Ozzy's favorite song when they were dating and first fell in love.
Current bands: Coldplay, Foo Fighters
Foods: French fries, milk shakes and ice

cream — even though she had a stomach banding operation for weight reduction in 1999. "I just eat little bits," she says.

Skincare products: Sisley

Pastime: Shopping

Sharon's Biggest Battle

Some might consider just being Mrs. Ozzy Osbourne a major trial in itself. But for Sharon, even through the ups and downs of Ozzy's drinking and substance abuse, love has conquered all. During their years together Sharon has been Ozzy's wife, confidant, best friend, playmate, and business partner. She was always there to smooth over the hazards that came their way. On July 1, 2002, right after the first season of MTV's *The Osbournes* wrapped, Sharon was diagnosed with cancer. If Sharon was shaken, Ozzy almost went to pieces, and was immediately at her side. The night before her July 3rd surgery, the two stayed up all night holding and comforting each other.

Ozzy explains: "She's my soulmate. . . . She's my whole world. . . . She has been my pillar of strength for many years." The news of Sharon's illness turned things around. Ozzy had to be the strong one — especially when post-surgery tests showed that the cancer had spread and Sharon was going to have undergo three months of chemotherapy. In typical Sharon style, she took it in stride and showed she even had more mettle than metal in her blood, saying, "I always knew how precious and lucky it is to be alive, and now even more so. I have a million more things I'm going to do. And I'm not going anywhere."

Kelly's Korner

Basics

Real name: Kelly Lee Osbourne
Birthday: October 27, 1984
Birthplace: England
Current residence: Beverly Hills, CA
Parents: Ozzy and Sharon Osbourne
Siblings: Aimee and Jack
Tattoo: A small pink heart on her left hip — her parents were not happy!

Celebrity best friend: Singer/actress Mandy Moore

Sharon's description: "Kelly has wobblers" — translation, Kelly can be very dramatic and have hissy fits.

Collections: Chairs, especially ones from the 1960s and 1970s

Education: Kelly left high school in California and earned her GED

Faves

Color: Pink

Bands: The Strokes, White Stripes, T-Rex, Blondie

CD: The Strokes' *Is This It*

Black Sabbath song: "Paranoid"

Recent concerts: Incubus

TV show: *The Brady Bunch*

Footwear: Her bunny slippers

Hair color: Electric pink (right now)

Chair: Her bubble chair, which hangs from her bedroom ceiling

Pastime: Shopping (she takes after her mom!)

School subjects: Science and history

Fashion designers: Zandra Rhodes, Helmut Lang
Stores: Barney's, Fred Segal
Kind of Boy: "I like smelly boys. I'm obsessed with the lead singer of the Strokes because he's a smelly rock star, and I love that."
Actors: Ewan McGregor, Matthew Lillard
City: New York

Just Jack

Basics

Real name: Jack Sabbath Osbourne
Birthday: November 8, 1985
Birthplace: England
Current residence: Beverly Hills, CA
Height: 5' 8"
Parents: Ozzy and Sharon Osbourne
Siblings: Kelly and Aimee
Sharon's description: "Jack is kind of the oddball at school."
Celebrity friends: Elijah Wood, pro skater Jason Dill

Most valuable book: A first edition of *Lord of the Rings*

Collections: Toothbrushes — he has one for every day of the week

Instrument: Drums

Career goal: Music producer — right now he is working with Epic Records as a talent scout and is developing the group Delusion.

Faves

Color: Black

Band: Tool — Jack has seen the band in concert over 20 times

CD: Tool's *Aenima*

Beatle album: *Revolver*

Black Sabbath song: "Sympton of the Universe"

Dog: Lola, the bull terrier

Fashion designers: Hurley, DVS shoes — both companies have made Jack a spokesman for them

Sport: Surfing — "I'm scared to death of eight-foot waves, and I try to paddled before they crash over me. But it's fun!"

Where Is Aimee?

Basics

Real name: Aimee Rachel Osbourne
Birthday: September 2, 1983
Birthplace: England
Parents: Ozzy and Sharon Osbourne
Siblings: Kelly and Jack
Career goal: A career in music
Surprise move: Aimee declined to be part of the first season of MTV's *The Osbournes*, and during the six months of filming she moved into the family's guesthouse. Don't be surprised if she shows up in the second season.
Sharon's description: "I think Aimee [is] the normal one in the family."
Fashion style: According to Kelly, Aimee is "preppy" — khaki pants and two-piece cardigan set and loafers.

Didja' Know?

- Ozzy's first band was named Approach.

- Heavy metal man Ozzy admits he likes Creed "because they can sing!"

- MTV paid the Osbournes $20,000 for each of the 13 episodes of the first season of their series. It's reported they will receive around $20 million for the second season. The second season takes place at their home in England, Welders House.

- There were 12 cameras in the house taping everything Ozzy and his clan did during the first season of *The Osbournes*.

- Ozzy's first job was as a plumber's assistant.

- Ozzy has a happy face tattooed on each knee to cheer him up when he wakes up in the morning.

- Sharon says she picked July 4th to be their wedding day so Ozzy would never forget it!

- At Ozzy's March 28, 1992 concert at Irvine Meadows in Laguna Hills, CA, the metal madman invited the audience to join him on stage — it caused $100,000 in damages.

- Sharon Osbourne was named one of *People* magazine's "50 Most Beautiful People" in May 2002.

- Ozzy was the Fox News Channel's guest of honor at the annual White House Correspondents Association dinner. President George W. Bush declared that Ozzy was his mother's favorite performer.

- Ten of Ozzy's 13 solo albums have gone multi-platinum.

- Jack has a teddy bear in his bedroom.

- Kelly still sucks her thumb when she sleeps.

- Ozzy had a hard time in school because he is severely dyslexic — but that was before doctors even understood the condition. Both Jack and Kelly are dyslexic.

- The Osbournes house includes a home theater, tropical design pool, Jacuzzi, and billiards room. The kitchen has four stoves, but they only use one.

- When Sharon travels she usually brings Maggie, one of her Japanese Chin dogs.

- Sharon called in a dog therapist named Tamara to work with their bullterrier, Lola, who would not be housebroken.

- Kelly gets embarrassed when Ozzy and Sharon snuggle and kiss in public. Why? "You're too old!" she tells her parents.

- The Osbournes have been looking to buy an apartment in New York City, but word has it that they've been turned down by several co-op and condo boards . . . maybe because of their high profile lifestyle!

- Sharon made the *London Times'* list of the 100 wealthiest women in Great Britain.

- On June 11, 2002, the Osbournes released

the CD, *The Osbourne Family Album*. Kelly made her singing debut with her cover rendition of Madonna's "Papa Don't Preach." It also includes:

* "Crazy Train" Pat Boone
* "Dreamer" Ozzy Osbourne
* "You Really Got Me" The Kinks
* "Snowblind" System of a Down
* "Imagine" John Lennon
* "Drive" The Cars
* "Good Souls" Starsailor
* "Mirror Image" Dillusion
* "Wonderful Tonight" Eric Clapton
* "Mama, I'm Coming Home" Ozzy Osbourne
* "Crazy Train" Ozzy Osbourne
* "Family System" Chevelle

• You can buy "The Osbournes" collectibles — from clothes to Bobble-Head dolls now. Sharon must approve every bit of merchandise.

• Ozzy got his star on the Hollywood Walk of Fame on April 12, 2002.

• Sharon might be getting a new dog — it's a

new breed and is the world's smallest dog. It's about the size of a grapefruit!

• Jack was once very into Shakespearean acting.

• Kelly never had a singing lesson before she recorded "Papa Don't Preach."

The First Ten Episodes — At a Glance

Did you catch 'em all? Here's a rundown of the Top Ten (okay, the first and only ten from season one) that kicked off *The Osbournes* phenom! All of them take place in Beverly Hills.

Episode One

The show started with an intro to the family: dad, aka Ozzy, mom Sharon, daughter Kelly, 16, and their son, Jack, 17. Viewers realized three things immediately: A) this is an unconventional family who truly loves one another B) why MTV uses those bleeping noises throughout the show, and C) this is a family worth checking out every week!

Episode Two

The dogs have gone "mad." Jack can't seem to control his favorite dog Lola. She soils the carpet and chews everything in sight. Mom Sharon has had enuff. She calls a dog psychologist. But the soiling persists.

Episode Three

Jack gets shipped off to summer camp, but returns because he doesn't fit in. And Kelly finally confesses to her parents that she's got a tattoo. Needless, to say Ozzy and Sharon are not pleased.

Episode Four

This is the one where the family has a "confrontation" with the neighbor and a ham was tossed over the fence.

Episode Five

Kelly and Mom go on a mega-shopping spree. And Ozzy freaks when Sharon books him for another show the following night. The Prince of Darkness seems to be furious. But all is forgotten when Ozzy is seen "rockin it up" on stage.

Episode Six

Ozzy and Sharon lay down the law with Kelly and Jack. They've been partying all-night and now they must pay — they've got a curfew.

Episode Seven

It's "turkey time" at the Osbournes. The family sits down for a Thanksgiving feast that includes stuffing, and name calling, all you would expect from this fun-loving bunch.

Episode Eight

Meet Jason Dill — Jack's skateboarder friend, who also happens to overstay his welcome at the Osbournes. But Jason isn't the only one in the doghouse. Lola (the dog) has been up to her old tricks again!

Episode Nine

'Tis the season to be Ozzy! Ozzy and the family celebrate the Christmas season. Yuletide style!

Episode Ten

Ozzy finally gets a star on the Hollywood Walk of Fame. The family beams with pride. The episode ends with a montage of clips from the season.

Rage — Real or Fake?

TV insiders can guess that the scene in episode five where Ozzy flies into a rage at Sharon in a Tucson hotel on the subject of a concert in Albuquerque the next night is an improvised comedy skit between the two great comedians who head the cast. Fake or real? Well, no performer who's been on the road for thirty-four years would wait until the night before playing a large city to complain about having to work too hard. And if you've lived to fifty-three, you've probably learned how to read an itinerary before the tour starts. But if someone like Ozzy were to pop his cork at his brilliant wife/manager, then it would probably have happened pretty much like episode five. Anyhow, it was funny as life and funny as comedy — an excellent combination.

CHAPTER ELEVEN
What Lies Ahead for the Osbourne Offspring?

The future for Kelly and Jack Osbourne is brighter these days than the Day-Glo colors of their hair. Just glance at a newsstand and you're bound to find their faces on the covers of several magazines. With at least two more seasons of *The Osbournes* secure under a multimillion dollar contract tooled by Sharon (thanks, Mom!), it's all these teenagers can do to keep up with the demand for them on the talk-show circuit. And along the way, America (and soon the world) is falling in love with its new It Girl and Boy.

Kelly's ivory skin, sweet smile, and genuine manner — not to mention her impeccable style *again* — have captured the hearts of people young and old. She's proven already that she's a natural in front of the camera and possesses the poise and grace to be a much-endeared television personality. Let's face it: She can even make us want to hear "Papa Don't Preach" again. Before recording the song, Kelly told the E! network, "I didn't choose the song. My mom did and asked me to do it. I'm kind of crapping myself because I don't think I'm a very good singer." But at the 2002 MTV Movie Awards, her performance was more hotly anticipated than bad-boy rapper Eminem's. She recorded the early Madonna hit with Incubus for *The Osbournes* soundtrack and is in talks with Epic Records about releasing a full CD. She'll also costar and sing in Disney's remake of *Freaky Friday*. Charming young Jack is well on his way to realizing many of his dreams: He's a talent scout for one of the industry's biggest labels, a coordinator of Second Stage at Ozzfest, and he's starting to set up his own record label. And he can play his drums. His passion for music and inherent gift for business as well as his social skills make him an heir apparent to both his mother's and grandfather's shoes as one of rock and roll's most powerful managers. Jack, the Hollywood supermogul? It's not hard to picture. Whether behind or in front of the scenes, one thing's for sure: With "hair like his," we know he's gonna be huge. Well, OK, the hair and the *charm*.

And More to Come . . .

With a soundtrack already in stores and a DVD box set of the first season inevitable, the merchandising craze of The Osbournes *is just beginning.*

Accessory Network has just been granted a license to produce and distribute an accessory collection that will include bags, CD cases, wallets, hosiery, a variety of novelty stationery items including notebooks, journals, diaries, pencil sets, and more.

Fans will have to wait until September, when The Osbournes collection will hit specialty stores and large retailers nationwide. Kids will be returning to school in the fall as colorful as the Osbournes themselves.

The hottest T-shirt of the moment:

"[BLEEP] My Family! I'm Moving in with the Osbournes."